THE LIBERTY BELL

The Sounds of Freedom

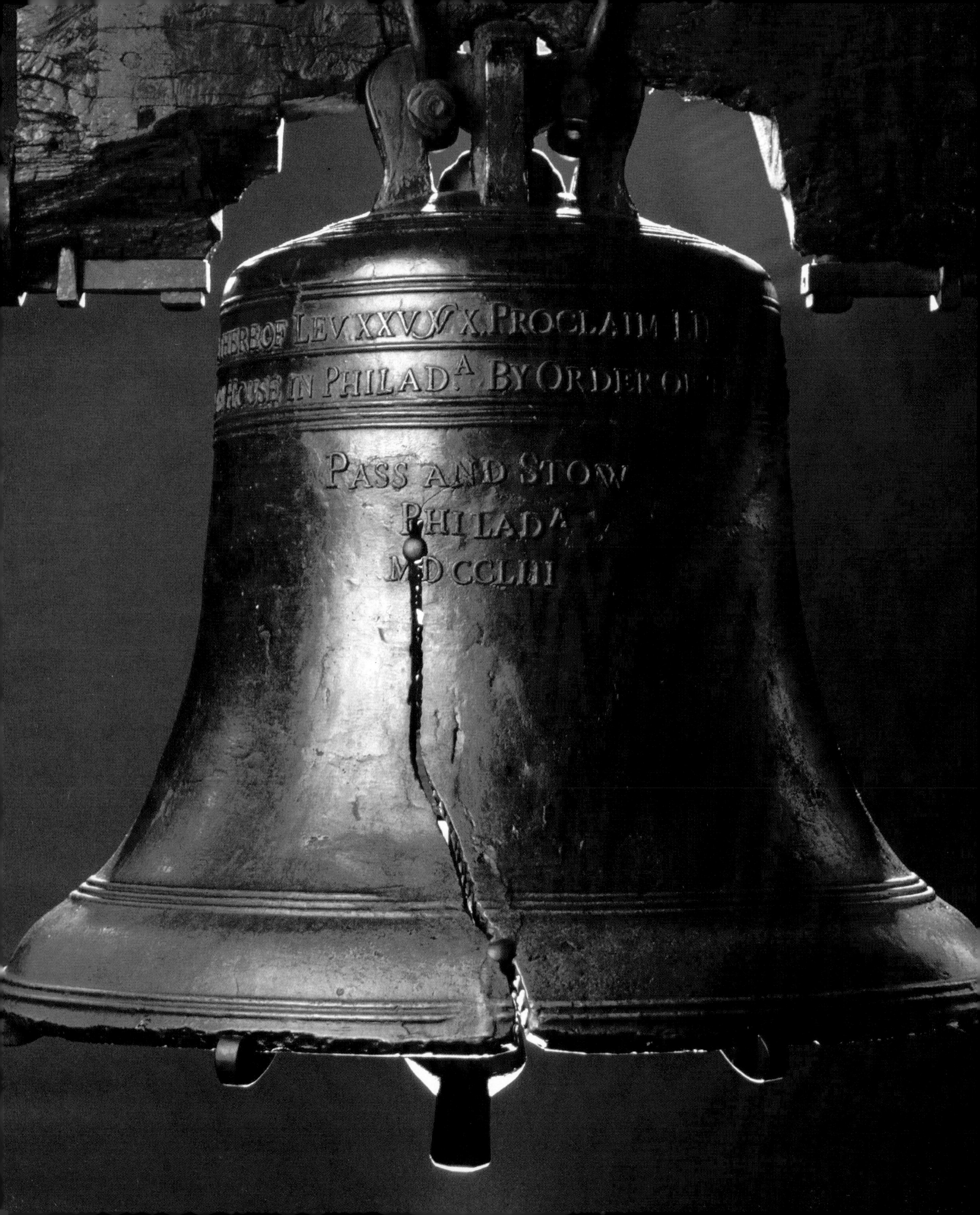
LEV. XXV. V X. PROCLAIM
IN PHILADA BY ORDER OF
PASS AND STOW
PHILADA
MDCCLIII

THE LIBERTY BELL

The Sounds of Freedom

The Liberty Bell weighs two thousand pounds, and it is twelve feet around at its bottom.

BY JON WILSON

8519563

GRAPHIC DESIGN
Robert A. Honey, Seattle

PHOTO RESEARCH
James R. Rothaus, James R. Rothaus & Associates

ELECTRONIC PRE-PRESS PRODUCTION
Robert E. Bonaker, Graphic Design & Consulting Co.

Library of Congress Cataloging-in-Publication Data
Wilson, Jon
The Liberty Bell : the sounds of freedom / by Jon Wilson
p. cm.
Summary: Describes the creation, history, and various locations
of the Liberty Bell and how it came to be a
symbol of the United States.
ISBN 1-56766-543-8 (library bound : alk. paper)

1. Liberty Bell — Juvenile literature.
[1. Libery Bell.] I. Title

F158.8.I3W55 1998   98-4332
973 — dc21   CIP
                                                               AC

CONTENTS

A DECLARATION OF INDEPENDENCE

This wood engraving by Davis Garber shows colonists gathering at Independence Hall on the eve of July 4, 1776.

In its early days, America was not a nation in its own right. Instead, it consisted of 13 **colonies**. The colonies were ruled by another country, England. Eventually, the colonists decided America was ready to stand on its own. Boldly, they wrote a **Declaration of Independence** in July of 1776. This declaration stated that the colonies would no longer be under British rule. At its first public reading, a bell rang from the tower of Independence Hall. The day was July 8, 1776, and the bell's ringing echoed across Philadelphia. The bell proclaimed freedom for the American people. It also marked the beginning of the War of Independence. This bell would someday be known as the Liberty Bell.

Bells are an important part of human history. The ancient Chinese used bells in their music and prayer. In the days of the Roman Empire, bells were used to announce public meetings. In the Middle Ages, during the time of castles, knights, and kings, bells announced births and deaths in the royal family. Bells are still used in clock towers to chime the time of day. Churches also use them to call people to religious services. Bells still sound out warnings of danger and ring cheerfully on days of celebration.

Right:
The Royal Palace bell in Bangkok, Thailand is suspended from an ornately carved tower.

Below, left:
Before newspapers, television, and radio, the town criers rang bells to get the people's attention when delivering the news.

Rupert Horrox/© Corbis

MAKING THE BELL—THREE TIMES!

The Liberty Bell was first made in 1751 by James Lester of the Whitechapel Bell Foundry in London. A **foundry** is a place where metal is melted and formed into new shapes. The bell cost about three hundred dollars. It was delivered to Philadelphia in August of 1752. But when the bell was tested, it broke! Two local men, John Pass and Charles Stow, melted down the broken bell and remade it. It broke during its second test, too. The men melted it down and made it again.

This foundry in Oxfordshire, England makes bells so large that in order for a man to adjust a clapper he must stand inside the bell.

This time the bell stood up to the test. The new bell was hung in the bell tower, or **belfry**, of Independence Hall. At first the bell was called the Old State House Bell. It was rung on all special occasions. In fact, neighbors sometimes complained about the constant ringing! Eventually, the name would change, but the bell would stand the test of time.

IN HIDING

In 1777 the 13 colonies were still fighting the British for independence. The British Army captured the city of Philadelphia. The British soon discovered that all the bells, including the Old State House Bell, had been hidden by the Americans. These loyal Americans, called **patriots**, knew that hiding the bells would help the American cause. Why? Because the British would have melted the bells and made them into cannons. In 1783, the Old State House Bell was finally brought from its hiding place. America had finally won its independence from British rule. The bell rang proudly to announce the victory.

An old woodcut shows the ringing of the Liberty Bell following the patriots' victory over the British.

Following the victory, Philadelphia became the new nation's capital. Independence Hall became the building where important government decisions were made. The Old State House bell rang on many special occasions. It rang on the Fourth of July, to announce birthdays or funerals of famous leaders, and during government meetings. The bell was right at the heart of the new nation.

Independence Hall in Philadelphia, Pennsylvania still attracts many visitors as seen in this 1974 photograph.

In 1839, a group of Americans called **abolitionists** wrote a poem about freedom and justice. Abolitionists were people working toward freedom for Africans who had been brought to America and kept as slaves. The poem was titled "The Liberty Bell." As far as anyone knows, it was the first time the Old State House Bell was called the "Liberty Bell." The poem was so moving and powerful that the new name stuck.

PUT TO REST

By 1846 the bell had been in service for 94 years. On February 22, it rang to celebrate George Washington's birthday. But the years had been hard on the Liberty Bell. By now it was cracked beyond repair. The nation's leaders decided to give this national treasure a rest. They removed the bell from the belfry of Independence Hall and put it into safe storage. A new, larger bell was hung in its place.

In 1852, there was a meeting of important leaders of the original colonies. The Liberty Bell was put on display in Independence Hall for the meeting. It sat in the same room where the nation's founders had signed the Declaration of Independence. The bell stood as a proud symbol of everything America had accomplished. This room became the bell's home for the next 124 years.

The east room in Independence Hall where the Declaration of Independence was adopted.

PENNSYLVANIA.—THE REMOVAL OF THE LIBERTY BELL FROM THE STATE HOUSE, PHILADELPHIA, EN ROUTE TO THE NEW ORLEANS EXPOSITION.—FROM A SKETCH BY A STAFF ARTIST.

The Liberty Bell was moved from the State House in Philadelphia to the New Orleans Exposition so that the large number of people attending the fair would have an opportunity to see the bell.

Over the next century, the Liberty Bell took many trips away from Independence Hall. Many Americans wished to see it, but few could afford the trip to Philadelphia. Instead, the bell was sent on a tour of major United States cities. People flocked to see it when it arrived in their city.

After the bell had been silent for 98 years, it was called out of retirement on June 6, 1944. World War II had been raging in Europe for many years. The United States was part of a final push to defeat Adolph Hitler and Nazi Germany. The final struggle was beginning in France, on the beaches of **Normandy**. The Liberty Bell rang out its call for freedom by radio. Afterward the bell was put to rest again. A recording of the Normandy broadcast still greets everyone who visits the bell.

On January 1, 1976, the United States began its 200th birthday celebration, called a **bicentennial**. As a part of the bicentennial, and in recognition of the bell's importance, a new building was constructed for it. The Liberty Bell Pavilion, 100 yards from Independence Hall, is the current home of this American treasure.

Buddy Mays/Corbis

Right:
The Liberty Bell stands as a symbol of American freedom.

Left:
The tower of Independence Hall first housed the Liberty Bell on June 7, 1753.

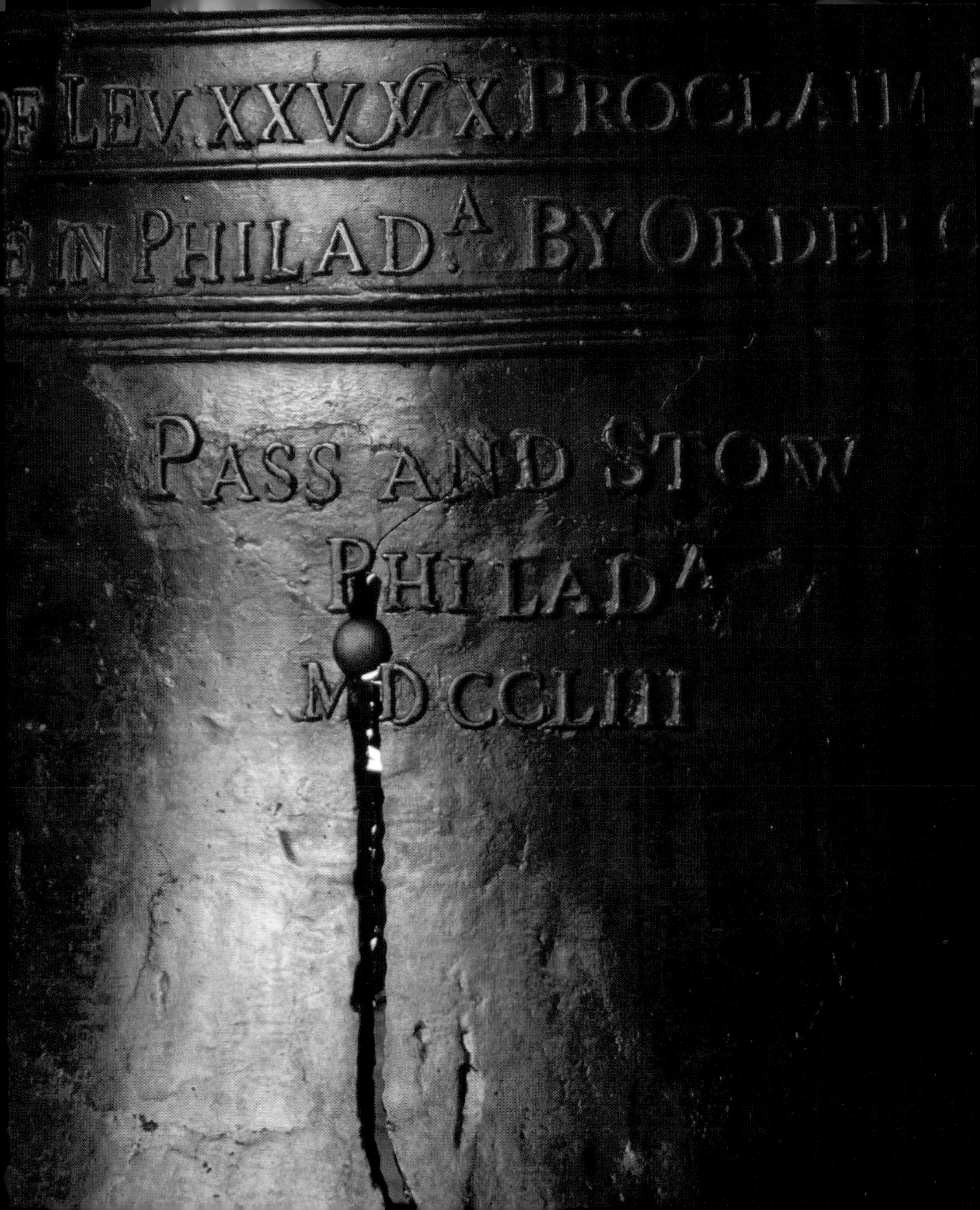

OF LEV. XXV. X. PROCLAIM

E IN PHILAD A. BY ORDER

PASS AND STOW

PHILAD A.

MDCCLIII

The people of the colony of Pennsylvania paid for making the bell. There are markings, or **inscriptions**, carved into the Liberty Bell. The top row reads "Proclaim liberty throughout all the land unto the inhabitants thereof. Lev. XXV. X." The end of this inscription refers to a passage from the Bible, Leviticus 25.10. The second inscription is, "By order of the Province of Pennsylvania for use in Philadelphia." Below that is a tribute to the men who made the bell, "Pass and Stow." The next line is an inscription honoring the people of Philadelphia. And finally, is the year the bell was made, "MDCCLIII," which are the roman numerals for 1753.

The bolt used to hold the bell together and part of the bell's inscriptions are seen here, close up.

Glossary

abolitionists (AB-oh-LIH-shun-ists)
Abolitionists were people who wanted to do away with the practice of slavery. An abolitionists' poem gave the Liberty Bell its name.

belfry (BELL-free)
A belfry is a room in which a bell is hung, often in a bell tower attached to a building. The Liberty Bell first hung in a belfry in Independence Hall.

bicentennial (BY-sen-TEN-ee-ull)
A bicentennial is a 200th birthday celebration. In 1976, the United States celebrated the 200th anniversary of the Declaration of Independence.

colony (KOLL-uh-nee)
A colony is an area that is ruled by a distant country. Before America became the United States, its 13 colonies were ruled by England.

Declaration of Independence (deck-le-RAY-shun of in-dee-PEN-dents) The United States's founders wrote the Declaration of Independence to state that they would no longer be ruled by England. The Liberty Bell rang at the declaration's first reading.

foundry (FOWN-dree)
A foundry is a place where metal is melted in hot furnaces and made into new shapes. The Liberty Bell was made first in a foundry in London, and then again in a foundry in Philadelphia.

inscriptions (in-SKRIP-shuns)
Inscriptions are words that are carved into something. Five different inscriptions are carved into the Liberty Bell.

Normandy (NOR-man-dee)
Normandy, on the northwestern coast of France, was where one of the most important battles of World War II was fought. The ringing of the Liberty Bell was sent out from Philadelphia by radio broadcast.

patriots (PAY-tree-uts)
Patriots are people who love their country and support its interests. In 1777, American patriots hid the Liberty Bell from British soldiers who had captured Philadelphia.

Index